Setting Goals

Pocket Mentor Series

The *Pocket Mentor* Series offers immediate solutions to common challenges managers face on the job every day. Each book in the series is packed with handy tools, self-tests, and real-life examples to help you identify your strengths and weaknesses and hone critical skills. Whether you're at your desk, in a meeting, or on the road, these portable guides enable you to tackle the daily demands of your work with greater speed, savvy, and effectiveness.

Books in the series

Becoming a New Manager

Coaching People

Creating a Business Plan

Delegating Work

Developing Employees

Dismissing an Employee

Executing Innovation

Executing Strategy

Giving Feedback

Giving Presentations

Hiring an Employee

Laying Off Employees

Leading People

Leading Teams

Making Decisions

Managing Crises

*Managing Difficult
   Interactions*

Managing Diversity

Managing Projects

Managing Stress

Managing Time

Managing Up

Negotiating Outcomes

Setting
Goals

Expert Solutions to
Everyday Challenges

Harvard Business Press

Boston, Massachusetts

Library of Congress Cataloging-in-Publication Data

  Setting goals : expert solutions to everyday challenges.
    p. cm. — (Pocket mentor series)
  Includes bibliographical references.
  ISBN 978-1-4221-2891-6 (pbk.)
  1. Goal setting in personnel management. 2. Management by objectives.
  HF5549.5.G6S48 2009
  658.3'01—dc22

                                                          2009025436

The paper used in this publication meets the requirements of the American National
Standard for Permanence of Paper for Publications and Documents in Libraries and
Archives Z39.48-1992.

Contents

Tips and Tools

Mentor's Message: Why Setting Goals Is Important

For any manager, setting goals—with your unit, with the individuals in it, and with peers and superiors—constitutes a major responsibility. Goals serve as beacons for managers and employees, guiding the actions they take every day on the job. Without goals, people can become directionless, floundering in the overwhelming "sea" of their organization and unsure of how to invest their time and energies.

But setting goals is challenging. How do you select objectives from the many possible goals you might define for and with your group, your employees, your peers, and yourself? This book walks you through the goal-setting process, providing ideas and practices for mastering the biggest challenges you'll encounter—such as making goals clear, defining an agenda for your group based on changes happening in your company or industry, identifying your top priorities when goals conflict, and building on your unit's strengths to successfully achieve the goals you've set.

Excel at setting goals, and you generate valuable results not only for your unit but also for your organization—in the form of more focused action, higher productivity, and greater efficiency on the job. Equally important, you'll win a reputation as a manager who knows how to establish a direction for your group and how to ensure that key business objectives are achieved. And that reputation can open numerous important doors as you advance in your managerial career.

Penny Locey, Mentor

Penny Locey directed leadership and organizational development for Polaroid Corporation as well as its career development programs and has consulted to profit and nonprofit organizations on performance management and team/management development and training. She was cofounder and director of the New England Institute for Career Development, an organization dedicated to professional growth of career management professionals. In addition to her private career consulting practice, she is a senior consultant for Keystone Associates, working with executives in career transition.

Linda A. Hill, Mentor

Linda A. Hill is the Wallace Brett Donham Professor of Business Administration at the Harvard Business School. She is the faculty chair of the Leadership Initiative and has chaired numerous HBS Executive Education programs, including the Young Presidents' Organization Presidents' Seminar and the High Potentials Leadership Program. She is a former faculty chair of the organizational behavior unit. She is the author of *Becoming a Manager: How New Managers Master the Challenges of Leadership* (2nd ed.).

Setting Goals: The Basics

What Is Setting Goals About?

oal setting is a formal process during which you define an agenda for your business unit, group, or team. This agenda may require you to collaborate with people outside your unit too—such as peers and people higher up in other parts of the organization.

When you set goals, you commit to outcomes that will be accomplished personally or through your team. Goal setting creates a long-term vision for your unit and provides the motivation to get you and others there. It has the additional benefit of helping you decide how you want to focus your resources and spend your time.

By setting goals and measuring their achievement, you generate enormous value for your organization. For example, you:

- Focus on what is most important to accomplish on a daily, weekly, and annual basis

- Provide a unified direction for your team

- Prioritize your workload and that of employees and others to focus on critical tasks

- Motivate your team and boost team members' overall job satisfaction

With these benefits of smart goal setting in mind, let's look more closely at what setting goals is all about—including types of goals, alignment of goals, prioritization of goals, and the top-down and bottom-up nature of goal setting.

Types of goals

As a manager, you are responsible for working with your team to set two types of goals:

- **Unit goals**—what your group as a whole will try to accomplish in a specific time period. For example, "Our goal is to redesign our Web site by the end of the year to make it easier to update customer information and to improve our customers' experience in doing business with us."

  Achieving some unit goals may require you and your employees to collaborate with people in other parts of the organization. For example, your group may need information or resources from another group to progress toward a goal. In these cases, you'll need to manage not only your employees but also your peers in other units whose help you need.

- **Individual goals**—how each employee will contribute to achieving the unit goals. For example, "Stefanie, our designer, will have the goal of creating a site that has a modular architecture but that is still attractive and compelling for online shoppers."

The person who makes a success of living is the one who sees his goal steadily and aims for it unswervingly. That is dedication.
   —Cecil B. Demille

Goal alignment

Unit and individual goals should emerge from the strategy of your company as a whole. For instance, if your organization's strategy is to become the industry's market-share leader through rapid product introductions, your unit and individual goals should serve that strategy. The table "Aligning Goals" shows examples of how different units might set goals supporting that strategy.

The real power of these cascading goals lies in their alignment with the objectives of the organization. Ideally, every employee

TABLE 1

Aligning goals

Company strategy: Become the market leader in rapid product introductions

Unit	Unit goal example	Individual goal example
Research and development	"Increase new-production introductions by 25% over the next 2 years"	"Product developers meet with marketing to discuss changes in consumer needs, to inform new-product development"
Marketing	"Leverage a wider range of types of media (such as social networking sites, the blogosphere, and massively multiplayer online games) to promote adoption of new offerings"	"Marketers conduct focus groups and other research into how consumers use these types of media to make product-purchasing decisions"
Manufacturing	"Retool manufacturing processes to allow for smaller and faster production runs of new products"	"Shop foreman retools one production line to serve as a pilot project for testing smaller, faster runs."

would understand his or her goal, how it relates to the unit's goals, and how the unit's activities contribute to the strategic objectives of the company.

Destiny is no matter of chance. It is a matter of choice: it is not a thing to be waited for, it is a thing to be achieved.
—William Jennings Bryan

Prioritization of goals

Goals differ in terms of *time frame* and *importance*. Regarding time frame: short-term goals are achievable within one or two months, and long-term goals are achievable over the course of several months or even years. This book focuses primarily on long-term goals. However, it's important to understand that tension can sometimes arise between short- and long-term goals. It's all too easy to put the more immediate (and thus seemingly more urgent) goals center stage, which can cause you to neglect the longer-term (and seemingly less urgent) goals.

Putting goals into categories can help you manage this balance. Consider these categories of goals, presented here in order of decreasing importance:

- **Critical goals** are crucial to your operation. They must be accomplished in order for your unit to continue running successfully or to remain competitive. For example, if you're a product manager, you would want to ensure that the technology used to process orders for a customized medical device is up-to-date so that your unit can get deliveries done on time.

- **Enabling goals** create a more desirable business condition or take advantage of a business opportunity. They are important, but they foster a better business environment over the long term rather than keeping your business on track and successful. For instance, if you head up a marketing team, you may set the enabling goal of capitalizing on a new fad diet to increase sales of a healthy snack food by 5 percent.

- **Nice-to-have goals** make improvements that enhance your business. They usually relate to making activities faster or easier. To illustrate, an environmental consultant creates a document to use as a template for completing field assessment reports.

Obviously, you should devote the lion's share of your unit's energies and resources to critical goals first, then enabling goals, and finally nice-to-have goals.

Top-down or bottom-up?

How are goals actually set in most organizations? It depends on the company's culture and management practices. The two most common methods of setting goals are *top-down* and *bottom-up*.

- **Top-down goal setting.** Each unit manager sets broad goals supporting the organization's strategy, and each employee is assigned objectives that are aligned with and support those broad goals. This approach is most appropriate with employees who need close supervision, who are new to your organization, or who aren't familiar with your unit's or organization's goals. In top-down goal setting, unit managers may also formulate goals that require coordination with other units.

- **Bottom-up goal setting.** Your direct reports develop individual goals, and you, their manager, integrate them into larger unit goals. This approach is most appropriate when your employees are fairly self-directed and clearly understand the business strategy and customer needs of the organization as a whole, as well as understanding their own roles within the unit and company. Bottom-up goal setting can also lead to goals that require coordination with people in other parts of the organization.

In most cases, however, a company's goals are determined through a process that includes both approaches. Usually, managers don't simply dictate objectives to employees without gathering their input, nor do employees have a free hand in determining their own goals without input from their supervisors. Instead, goals are determined through joint decision making in which managers, their peers, and employees discuss what is necessary to support the company's aims and what is feasible for everyone to achieve.

"SMART" Goals

egardless of whether your unit's and employees' goals are set through a top-down process, a bottom-up one, or both, it is important that they be expressed clearly. In fact, significant business value comes from expressing the original broad idea in specific terms, since the target often changes as the desired outcomes become clear. The more explicitly you state goals from the beginning, the more likely people will be able to agree on whether or not the goals have been achieved. Five criteria—commonly known by the acronym "SMART"—can help you state your goals clearly and explicitly. We examine these criteria next.

What makes a goal "SMART"?

As you set both unit and individual goals, you'll want to write them down. Doing so can help you more clearly define what you hope to accomplish, and it strengthens your and your employees' commitment to reaching the goals. Use the following five "SMART" criteria to draft clear goals:

- **Specific.** You can describe the details of what must be accomplished to achieve the goal.

- **Measurable.** You can measure the goal using either quantitative assessments (for example, number of new customers or number of new products introduced) or qualitative assessments (for instance, higher workforce morale).

- **Achievable.** You and your employees can achieve the goal.

- **Realistic.** The goal is realistic, given existing constraints, such as time and resources available to devote to accomplishing the goal.

- **Time-limited.** You must achieve the goal within a specified time frame.

The table "SMART versus Not-So-SMART" shows examples of how goals might meet these five criteria.

TABLE 2

SMART versus not-so-SMART goals

SMART goal	Not-so-SMART goal
Add 20 new systems engineers in the next 3 years who are capable of handling the new advanced programming language—year 1: add 2 new people, year 2: add 9 new people, year 3: add 9 new people.	Add systems engineers who are capable of handling the new advanced programming language. (This goal is not **s**pecific, **m**easurable, or **t**ime-bound.)
Raise sales 10% annually over the next 3 years.	Improve sales over the next year. (This goal is not **s**pecific or **m**easurable.)
Reduce average duration of customer service phone calls by 30% over the next 2 years.	Reduce average duration of customer service phone calls by 50% over the next year. (This goal is not likely **a**chievable or **r**ealistic.)

What Would YOU Do?

Torn Between Ten Teams

ARGIE WAS HAVING a tough time managing her product development group. Team members were frustrated because they were being pulled in a hundred different directions: The customer service team needed a bunch of different documents laying out product features and benefits. The team responsible for marketing needed to know how various new offerings differed from competing companies' products. Finance was waiting for a report on various product's potential profits and losses that should have been submitted a week ago. Amid all these different requests, Margie's group was supposed to release a new product in just two months!

It was simply too much. Margie could tell that morale in her group was low and that her direct reports were feeling overworked, overwhelmed, and underappreciated. How could she get the group to focus on what they were trying to achieve, rather than on the challenges that were being thrown at them along the way? How could she use effective goal setting to get her group back on track?

What would YOU do? The mentors will suggest a solution in *What You COULD Do.*

"Spotlight on the Importance of Achievability" describes how one executive views the SMART criterion of achievability for setting goals.

Spotlight on the Importance of Achievability

Companies must respond to competition and change by deciding how best to use their resources to achieve their overall goals. Executives lead the process by setting a clear, achievable strategy that unit managers must then execute by defining and achieving specific goals supporting that strategy. Here's how Roger Parry, chairman of Clear Channel International, described the importance of setting clear and achievable goals:

Some years ago I was working in an advertising agency group and was responsible for one of the public relations businesses we'd recently acquired. The chief executive told us that he wanted this business to double its sales within two years. Now, the problem with doubling your sales within two years in a business like that is that you have to go and hire people to do the work. The constraint actually wasn't winning new clients; the constraint was hiring people, because at the time there was a great shortage. So we went away from that annual budget review knowing in advance that we were going to fail because it wasn't going to be possible to hire that number of people sufficiently quickly. But the same goal had been set for all the businesses across the whole group, so we were stuck with something we couldn't possibly achieve.

If what went wrong was the original process of setting the goal, everyone has to admit to that and be realistic about it. If you don't have that sort of postmortem, the problem you'll face is that you'll get so many disaffected members of staff that your whole organization becomes dysfunctional. There will be a lot of people working, feeling a sense of failure. It is very important that people feel a sense of success. That does not mean that you always set goals that are so easy that everyone achieves them. It's not like an examination process where everybody passes; but the important thing is that where a goal is missed, it's missed for reasons that everyone understands and you can genuinely say: "That was force majeure; that was an external unexpected event." It shouldn't be missed because the original goal was so unrealistic that it couldn't be done.

Clear goals for a business manager come as a result of really understanding the environment within which they're operating, and also as a result of a dialogue between that business manager and his or her chief executive. The right goals are those that both parties understand and buy into, rather than something that just sounds like a very good number to talk about to your shareholders.

Quantitative versus qualitative goals

As you write down your goals, you will notice that many of them can be *quantitatively* measured. For example, your goal may be to increase sales in a region by 10 percent in the next quarter.

Some goals, however, are not so easily measured, such as goals related to professional development, workforce morale, or customer satisfaction. These are *qualitative* goals. For example, an employee may want to increase her comfort level with speaking in a public forum. She may set a quantitative goal of making six public presentations in the upcoming year. But how can you assess whether she actually is more comfortable speaking to large audiences after completing these six presentations (a qualitative goal)? You might begin by scheduling a follow-up discussion with her after each presentation to evaluate how she felt and to discuss possible improvements.

A goal properly set is halfway reached.
—Abraham Lincoln

Achievement of qualitative goals is more subjective and therefore difficult to measure. However, don't shy away from establishing such goals—for yourself and for your employees—even though they may be harder to evaluate than quantitative goals. Qualitative goals are just as important as quantitative ones, because they challenge people to improve and can ultimately help them strengthen valuable skills.

Also, an overemphasis on quantitative goals to the exclusion of qualitative ones can cause people to misidentify what's most important. For example, suppose that all people saw were quantitative goals about increasing sales. In this case, they might focus so much on reaching those numbers that they neglect other equally important goals that are qualitative, such as improving what it's like for customers to do business with the company. While sales can be readily measured, customers' experiences with the company (such as how pleasant a service rep was or how easily a product was ordered) can be less easily measured. But they might be just as important to the company's strategy.

What You COULD Do

Remember Margie's concern about how to use effective goal setting to get her product development group back on track?

Here's what the mentors suggest:

Even though Margie and her group are overworked, she needs to step back and prioritize all the work they have to accomplish. Since releasing the new product on time is, in all likelihood, the highest priority, Margie should focus her team's efforts on achieving this key goal. The requests from customer service, marketing, and finance will need to be either delegated to someone else or postponed until someone in her group has free time. By setting this goal and making it a priority, Margie will be able to focus the energy of her group on one objective and provide a unified direction for all her employees.

Defining Goals
for Your Unit

As a manager, you are surrounded by potential goals you might set for and with your unit. In a typical day, you probably think about how your unit could operate more smoothly, what new responsibilities you may want to take on, and how your staff could work better as a team and with peers from other units. Each one of these areas could have associated goals. Your challenge is to sort through all the potential goals you could pursue and identify those that will create the most value for your unit and your organization. The following suggestions can help.

Identifying potential goals

On a regular basis (usually once or twice a year for most organizations), review your unit's diverse activities and your team's roles. Look for opportunities to draft goals in areas that will make the greatest impact. Bring your team together to brainstorm possible unit goals by exploring questions such as:

- What initiatives do we need to accomplish to support our company's strategy? Is that strategy changing? If so, what does that suggest for our goals?

- What standards are we striving for in the work we produce in our unit?

- What improvements in our unit's productivity and efficiency will generate the most positive impact for our organization overall?

- What benefits do we want to give to our customers? Which benefits must we give them to become more competitive or to remain just as competitive as we are now?

- Are the required specifications for our products and services changing? If so, how can we respond as a unit?

- What's happening in our industry and with our competitors that might be important to address in the goals we're setting?

During this brainstorming phase, don't worry about time constraints or potential problems with executing a goal that someone thought of during your brainstorming session. You'll narrow down your list of potential goals later by considering such constraints.

Also, don't forget to list potential goals that might need to be defined as a result of pressure from your customers or changes in your organization's environment. For example, are distribution or manufacturing technologies changing radically in your industry? If so, what unit goals might help you take advantage of those changes to enhance your company's success? "Tips for Setting Unit Goals" provides additional quick reference points for this process.

Prioritizing and selecting goals

Once you and your team have generated a list of potential goals, your next step is to narrow down the list to only those objectives

Tips for Setting Unit Goals

- Focus on the business strategy, customers, and your unit's performance.
- Keep a running list of possible goals to consider when brain-storming your goal list.
- Make sure that your unit goals align with your own manager's objectives and your organization's intentions.
- Keep unit goals SMART (specific, measurable, achievable, realistic, and time-limited).
- Write your unit goals down and keep the list visible for everyone in your group.

that your unit will commit to pursue. Start by asking questions to help you distinguish high-priority goals from low-priority ones. For example:

- Which goals on this list does our organization value the most?

- Which goals could provide the most leverage for our team to generate the most valuable business results?

- Which goals will position us to exert the greatest impact on performance and profitability in our unit?

While you're exploring such questions, you might also look through the list for goal ideas that could be consolidated into one larger goal for your unit. For instance, if several people proposed goals related to new uses of different types of media to create more effective marketing messages, you might put these together into one goal.

Next, review your brainstormed list of goals and use your criteria to rank them as priority A, B, or C. Here's what these rankings mean.

- **Priority A.** These goals have high value and primary importance. For example, they directly support your company's strategy and will deliver major improvements in business results.

- **Priority B.** These goals have medium value and secondary importance. That is, they may not align quite as strongly with your organization's strategy, and perhaps they'll produce less crucial business results.

- **Priority C.** These goals have lesser value or little urgency. Perhaps they're nice-to-have goals that have indirect relevance to your company's strategy or unit function.

Setting goals sometimes means asking not only "What goals are we going to commit to?" but also "What goals are we *not* going to pursue?" You might want to drop some goals from your list because they have less value or urgency, or because there is limited time, money, or other resources to support the goal. (Sometimes, goal setting involves making trade-offs.)

With these realities in mind, you'll want to eliminate all priority C goals. Then, look again at your priority B goals. Reassign them as either priority A or priority C; they are either worth your unit's time or not. The goals that now remain on your list are your top-priority goals.

Since resources are usually limited, you must prioritize what you will try to accomplish once again: as a last step, review your priority A goals separately and rank them according to importance. Be careful not to let any short-term goals on the list automatically take precedence over long-term ones.

Finally, write down your final, ordered priority A list. Periodically reassess your list to ensure that it continues to be consistent with your organization's and unit's priorities.

"Steps for Identifying and Prioritizing Unit Goals" provides a handy reference for how to define goals for your unit.

Steps for Identifying and Prioritizing Unit Goals

1. Once or twice a year, review your unit's diverse activities and your team's roles, looking for possible high-value goals. Include relevant customers, team members, and your manager in the goal-setting process.
2. Identify criteria for prioritizing your goals. For example, which goals will contribute the most to revenue growth?
3. Review your list of goals and use your criteria to rank them as A-, B-, or C-level priority.
4. Reassign your priority B goals into priority A or priority C; they are either worth your time or not. The goals that are now on your priority A list are your final goals.
5. Review your priority A goals separately and rank them according to importance.
6. Goals on the priority C list can be delegated, put on the back burner, or discarded.

Defining Goals
for Individuals

I n addition to defining goals for your unit, you need to set goals with the individuals who make up your unit—that is, goals for each of your employees and for yourself. Setting individual goals is part of the goal-aligning and -cascading process we explored earlier. In the following pages, we present ideas and practices for handling this part of the goal-setting process.

Clarifying individual goals

Each of your direct reports will need to establish individual goals that reflect the overall goals that you and your employees have defined for your unit. Your role is to support and assist your employees in this process. At the end of the goal-setting process, individual employees should be able to say (without prompting) something like:

"Our company's goal is to _____. My unit's contribution to that goal is to _____. And my part in this effort is to _____."

As we've seen, individual goals may involve collaboration with people in other parts of the organization, if your employees need information or other resources from peers in other units in order to reach their goals.

To clarify individual goals, make sure that all your team members understand the unit's goals, their specific roles within the unit, and your expectations for them. Ask each person to use the

SMART criteria to draft—or to modify—a set of goals for him- or herself. Together, make decisions about the details on commitments to particular goals, including your role in supporting each goal's achievement.

For example, points to be discussed may include deadlines for achievement of specific goals, the actual results you expect achievement of a goal will produce, and resources or managerial time that you'll provide an employee for the purpose of accomplishing a particular goal. You might also discuss with the person what will happen if something goes wrong while he or she is working toward the goals you've defined. That is, what's the fallback or contingency plan?

Remember to tie progress toward achieving goals to performance evaluation, develop clear descriptions of expected output, and confirm that everyone knows who is responsible and accountable for each goal's achievement.

Ensuring successful achievement of goals

Your team members will be most likely to achieve the individual goals you and they have defined if the following conditions are in place:

- Each person agrees with you on his or her specific goals and the outcomes required.

- You establish clear checkpoints for progress toward the goals and designate time to provide feedback to employees on what they are doing well that they can generalize or replicate, and how they can make midcourse corrections.

- Team members have the resources, appropriate skills and knowledge, and authority to accomplish their goals.

- Individuals understand how their ability to meet their individual goals will affect the unit's overall goals.

- You recognize and acknowledge when employees have achieved their individual goals.

"Tips for Setting Your Team Members' Goals" provides additional ideas for managing this aspect of setting goals.

Tips for Setting Your Team Members' Goals

- Give as much control and input as possible to your staff in developing their own goals. Be especially sensitive to time-frame suggestions.
- Tie goal achievement to performance evaluation; this will demonstrate to your employees how much you value achievement of their individual goals.
- Once you have agreed to a goal for an individual employee, set up adequate resources and authority for the person to carry out the goal. Make sure that others (such as your own manager and the individual employee's peers) are supportive too.
- Encourage your staff to consider goals that require them to acquire additional training. That will enable them to gain important new skills. Follow through on getting them trained.
- Let your staff decide how they'd like achievement of their individual goals to be recognized. Recognition tailored to your employees' preferences is much more powerful than recognition dictated from "on high."

Setting goals for yourself

As a manager, you need to establish individual goals for yourself, in addition to goals for your direct reports. These may include:

- Unit goals, or components of unit goals, that require your specific skills or unique perspectives based on your experience—and that you therefore cannot delegate to others.

- Goals that reflect your contributions to your team members' individual goals ("Select a new training program that my customer-service staff needs to meet their goal of increasing customer loyalty by 10 percent").

- Goals that involve communicating your unit's activities throughout the broader organization (for instance, "Circulate project status reports to management team every week instead of every month").

- Goals that require securing resources for your team ("Hire two new temps by end of the month who can take on admin tasks and free up team members to focus on their goals").

- Goals that entail integrating the unit's goals with those of other units ("Start meeting weekly with peer managers to understand their units' objectives and challenges").

You may even find that your role within your company warrants creating goals that are not specifically related to your unit. You might decide, for example, to serve on a cross-functional task force or assist in community-relations activities for your company. Tying goals to these responsibilities will help ensure that you follow through with the commitments you have made that lie outside your unit responsibilities.

Work with your own manager to reach agreement on your individual goals, to build a shared understanding of the expected outputs of these goals, and to secure the support and training that you will need to be able to achieve them. In addition, make sure to communicate your individual goals to your team members. If they understand your priorities and how the team's activities fit into those priorities, that understanding will help all of you work together more smoothly.

Maximizing
Goal Success

efining goals clearly (whether they're for your unit or for individuals in your unit) isn't enough to ensure successful achievement of the goals. You also need to establish an environment in which everyone is as motivated and enabled as possible to reach the unit and individual objectives that have been defined. How to foster such an environment? In the following pages, we'll explore some valuable suggestions.

Establishing a sense of ownership

You and your employees must see your goals as important and worthy of effort; otherwise, you will lose your motivation when you hit obstacles. One way to achieve this sense of commitment is to involve your employees in setting goals and determining how to achieve them. This gives employees a sense of ownership over the goals you've set together and will help them hold each other accountable for the end result.

Begin by discussing corporate goals and how your unit can help realize them. Explain why you are selecting challenging goals and why achieving them is so important for both the organization and your team. Make sure people see a personal benefit, too, such as greater visibility in the organization, a bonus if unit goals are met, skills development, or nonmonetary rewards that your team members value (such as certificates to restaurants, or company-funded trips for employees and their families). This approach will build awareness of how your goals align with organizational strategy and demonstrate to employees the importance of what you are asking them to do.

Defining achievable, challenging goals

Part of your task in setting unit and individual goals is balancing achievability with ambition. You want to set goals that are possible to meet, but that also "stretch" and excite people, infusing them with the sense that there's a challenge to meet.

This is a delicate balance: if the goals you've set are *too* ambitious, you run the risk that people won't be able to accomplish them. Not only can this can be embarrassing for you and your employees; it can also have more serious repercussions. For example, frustration or demotivation can result if you have to reduce an employee's bonus because he or she missed a target. Your team members are also likely to resent you if you set goals that are not achievable.

At the same time, you don't want to aim too low. If you are overly cautious—setting goals that can be reached very easily—you will miss opportunities and end up with mediocre performance. Starting with focused goals that you can later expand into larger, more ambitious ones may help you achieve the right balance.

"Spotlight on Ambitious Goals" provides one leader's perspective on the value of setting ambitious objectives for your unit and employees.

Spotlight on Ambitious Goals

Don't be afraid to instigate a radical step change to alter the direction of a business. Setting ambitious goals can trigger entrepreneurial thinking, create improved performance, and significantly increase shareholder value. Here's how Stephen Dando, group HR director at Reuters, described a situation in which setting ambitious, transformational goals helped his business improve its performance:

There are times when it's appropriate to evolve, but there are times when you need to bring about step change. One device you can use for getting there is to redefine the level of ambition so dramatically that people are almost forced to think from a blank sheet of paper rather than the incremental way that most of us have learned to think about performance.

Diageo was the merger of Guinness and Grand Met, two very well-established companies coming together. While they were both great companies, relatively speaking, they had both underperformed against stock market expectations over a period of time. I think one of the questions the investment community was probably asking itself was why they should believe that bringing together these two companies would suddenly result in superior performance. Our then chief executive quickly declared on behalf of everyone that we were going to *double total shareholder return within a four-year period.* That signified a dramatic improvement in the company's performance. This was beyond the track record and performance experience of either of the two companies. I was really struck by the impact that that had. There was an initial period when a lot of us thought that this was a slightly mad thing to have done. How on earth were we going to deliver targets? The business targets were just so aggressive that it was hard to see how we could make it work.

But what was interesting was seeing how people's approach to that challenge changed over time. As people digested what that meant, what became very clear was that incrementalism was never going to get you there. Trying a bit harder with the business strategies or approaches that you had was never going to get you there. The trajectory in terms of business performance had changed so dramatically that the only way you had a chance of getting there was to completely rethink the way that you approached your business.

Focusing on targets

Starting off with small, specific targets is another way to motivate your team members to keep forging ahead toward their goals. Many managers try to get their people to do too much too quickly and fail to focus on one or two sharply defined targets. It is nearly impossible to succeed when you establish vague or overly broad goals.

Consider the example of a management team at a newspaper publishing plant that tried to institute a comprehensive quality-improvement effort. The team accomplished very little because the company's needs were so great and employees were focused in many different directions.

After this failed attempt, the team then worked with production managers to target a specific, achievable goal: reducing the number of typographical errors in the company's products. With this clear focus, they ultimately succeeded. They were then able to repeat the process they used and apply it in identifying and accomplishing additional, more ambitious goals.

> *The world makes way for the man who knows where he is going.*
> —Ralph Waldo Emerson

Determining performance metrics

Another way to maximize the probability that your people will achieve their goals is to determine performance metrics. That is, what will happen if a goal is achieved? How will you *know* it's been achieved? Too many managers state goals in vague terms; for example: "We will reorganize our systems to make the customer our top priority." When it comes time to evaluate achievement of this particular goal, it would be difficult to say whether the goal had been met.

A better way to state the same goal would be to express it in terms of specific desired performance: "We will redesign the entire customer service process. If we are successful, 95 percent of customer calls will be handled by a single service rep, and 80 percent of all calls will be resolved in three minutes or less."

Performance metrics are important, but be careful not to get *too* caught up in evaluating your employees exclusively on these metrics. For example, if telephone operators are judged *only* on whether their calls last three minutes or less, you may be unwittingly encouraging them to provide quick answers that aren't in the customer's best interests.

Assigning responsibility

Once you and your employees agree on a set of measurable goals, make it clear who is responsible for each component. Like the suggestions discussed earlier, this one will help increase the chances that people will achieve their goals. If you don't explicitly assign responsibility for specific goals, your employees may "delegate" it upward (that is, look to *you* to achieve the goal), especially if you're also involved in the project.

Consider the example of Marie, president of a company whose customers were complaining about bugs in its new software product. Marie set a goal of eliminating 90 percent of the bugs in the following quarter. She met with the heads of the development, design, and quality assurance departments, and each claimed that his or her group was doing its job and that the quality problems were originating in a different department. After spending many hours talking with these managers, Marie was not successful in making changes in any of the departments. She knew that without a change, the next release of the product would still have a significant number of bugs.

The turnaround came when she told her department heads that she thought it was unwise for her to try to come up with a solution to the quality issue by herself. Instead, she gave her direct reports the full responsibility for reducing the bugs. She assigned to one executive the responsibility for developing a comprehensive plan to achieve the necessary quality improvements. She then requested that each of the other managers produce a plan with a time table for his or her unit's contribution toward achieving the goal. Using these plans, the department heads were successful in reducing the number of bugs in the subsequent product release.

"Tips for Increasing Goal Success" provides additional ideas for sweetening the odds that you and your employees will accomplish the goals you've set.

Tips for Increasing Goal Success

- Spend priority time on completing the tasks that relate directly to your goals.
- Do not allow priority C goals to creep onto your priority A list.
- Work with goals that are compatible with one another. Conflicting goals compete for your attention.
- Make your goals known to others who can help directly or be supportive.
- Be persistent. Remind yourself of the payoff when you hit snags.
- Take the time to celebrate after reaching critical milestones.

Accomplishing
Your Goals

Y ou've read about how you can set goals effectively with your unit and the individuals in it, and how to create conditions that enable people to achieve the goals you've set. You can further increase the chances that people will achieve their goals by applying specific practices while you and your team are "executing on" the goals—that is, working toward achieving them. The following recommendations can help.

Pursuing the goals you've defined

To make goals achievable, you need to break them down into actual tasks, plan the execution of those tasks, and follow your plan. Use this process for achieving unit and individual goals:

1. Identify the key goals.

2. Ask, "What specific tasks will have to be done in order to accomplish each goal?"

3. Determine which tasks need to be completed sequentially and put those in order. If there are tasks that can be completed simultaneously, incorporate them into your plan accordingly.

4. For each key task, describe the results or outcomes desired.

5. Determine what resources (money, people) are needed to carry out each task.

6. Establish a time frame for the completion of each task. Include a start and finish date.

7. Set up milestones along the way to review progress and overall impact. Make sure to include what you expect to achieve by each milestone.

"Planning for a Goal" gives an example of how Ted, a manager of a sales force, used this process with one unit goal he had defined.

Planning for a Goal

Ted had set numerous goals for his group, the sales force for a small but growing pet-products company. One of the goals was "Increase sales of pet accessories 10 percent by year end." The tasks required to accomplish this goal included selling accessories in a broader array of channels, such as veterinarians' offices, brick-and-mortar pet stores, online stores (pet-related and nonpet-related), and grocery stores. Ted determined that these tasks could be accomplished in parallel rather than in a particular sequence, and he laid out specific results he wanted to see his salespeople achieve with each task (for example, "a 5 percent increase in sales of accessories to veterinarians' offices within six months").

Ted also determined the resources needed to carry out these tasks, which included hiring several new sales representatives. And he set up milestones for reviewing progress, such as "Every two weeks, let's take stock of how things are going on each goal." Thanks to his ability to follow this disciplined process as his group pursued its goals, the sales force was able to achieve almost all of the unit goals that Ted had defined.

Managing obstacles

By anticipating obstacles you and your people may encounter while pursuing goals, you can more easily surmount those obstacles and continue making progress toward your goals.

Before you begin executing plans toward a particular goal, consider the potential problems that might confront each goal and its associated projects. For example, could funding for a needed project dry up? Might a key employee leave the unit or company? Could a task turn out to take much more time than you originally expected? Might people begin losing enthusiasm for the goal?

Then, map out possible solutions for defeating each obstacle. The following strategies may be helpful:

- If your team members are having trouble completing their tasks, perhaps they are losing their motivation to achieve one or more goals. Revisit the payoff that will come with achievement of the goal, and remind yourself and your team why all of you are dedicated to the goal(s).

- Line up your resources before committing to a goal. Make sure you have committed people in place so staffing gaps will not become an obstacle. Make sure other resources (time, equipment, money) are also sufficient to achieve the goal.

- If you find you are paralyzed by the risks associated with a goal, evaluate the probability that the risks will occur. Risks that have little probability of happening can be set aside. List the benefits of overcoming a particularly unnerving risk, to help restore your courage and ability to move forward.

If a task seems overwhelming, break it down into smaller subtasks. And from the outset, keep in mind that the process of working toward a goal has natural stops and starts: There will be times when required resources are lined up and ready to go, so you can move forward toward accomplishing the goal. There are other times when you need to wait for someone else to complete a task before you can continue working toward the goal. There are also periods when tasks become difficult or tedious, and other times when they flow easily. During frustrating and difficult times, stay focused on the payoffs you'll generate (for yourself, your unit, and your organization) by sticking with it and achieving the goal.

> *Obstacles are those frightful things you see when you take your eyes off the goal.*
> —Henry Ford

Monitoring and communicating progress

As you and your employees move toward achieving the goals you've set, it's vital to continually monitor progress and communicate updates to people as needed to stay on track. For example, do you know whether your sales team is ahead of or behind schedule in achieving a particular sales-increase goal? Is the Web-site task force moving forward according to plan, or has it become mired in some technical problem?

Monitoring generates the knowledge you need to modify tasks, contingency plans, and follow-up criteria, and to communicate these midcourse adjustments to everyone involved in working toward a goal. You (or a project manager reporting to you) must:

- Update everyone involved as you make progress toward each goal

- Review the upcoming projects and required resources

- Check off completed projects as you reach milestones

- Revise completion dates, when necessary

- Record actual completion dates for future reference if you change the dates originally committed to

- Review the impact on later tasks, and adjust those accordingly

"Steps for Monitoring Your Progress" offers additional actions you can take to stay on top of things as you and your people work toward a goal.

Achieving your aims

These additional strategies can further help maximize the odds that you and your direct reports will reach the unit and individual goals you've established:

- Share your goals with colleagues and friends. In addition to being supportive, they may have ideas on how to accomplish them.

- Focus on goals that will give you and others the greatest sense of accomplishment.

Steps for Monitoring Your Progress

1. Work from your own daily and weekly schedules, and from your team's overall work plan. Check off completed tasks as they occur.
2. As you reach milestones, review upcoming tasks and required resources.
3. As you progress, update everyone involved in achieving the goals.
4. Step back periodically and assess whether your goals are still realistic, timely, and relevant.
5. If reaching any of the goals no longer creates value, revise that goal. However, be sure to get buy-in from your team, upper management, and other involved groups before you do.
6. When you feel you have reached a goal, confirm that others agree that the goal has been accomplished and the desired impact achieved.
7. Identify what was successful and what you would change in the future for each completed goal. Record both and communicate your lessons learned to everyone involved.

- Devote most of your time to completing the tasks that relate to your most important goals.

- Be persistent about working toward your goals. Remind yourself of the payoff when you hit snags.

- Be flexible about *how* you accomplish your goals. For example, be willing to revise your unit's project list to reflect changes in your situation such as a reduction in the project budget or the unexpected departure of a key employee. Have a backup plan in case something goes wrong while you're working toward a goal.

- Don't be afraid to ask for help from upper management, direct reports, or other stakeholders.

- Finally, when you have achieved a goal, take the time to celebrate with your team. Be sure to reward yourself and your team members appropriately.

"Steps for Accomplishing Your Goals" provides further ideas for ensuring that the goals you've defined are reached.

Steps for Accomplishing Your Goals

1. Break each goal down into specific tasks and (if necessary) subtasks.
2. Sequence tasks that must be completed in a particular order. Distinguish these sequential tasks from those that can be carried out in parallel.
3. For each key task, describe the results or outcomes you expect the task to deliver.
4. Determine what resources are needed to carry out each task and make sure that you have them available. For example, do you have the money to get the job done? Do you have people with the necessary training to complete the task?
5. Establish a time frame for the completion of each task. Include a start and finish date. You may want to use a Gantt chart or

some other time-scaled task diagram to make your schedule clear to your team.

6. Set up milestones along the way to review project completion and overall impact. Make sure to include what you expect to achieve by each milestone.

7. Consider the potential obstacles that might confront each goal and its associated task. Map out possible solutions for each obstacle.

Evaluating Goals You've Set

W hile you're working toward a goal and after you've achieved it, evaluating the goals you've defined and accomplished is helpful. That way, you can modify goals in midstream if necessary to accommodate new realities. And you can draw lessons that can then be applied to your next experience in working toward a goal. The intent behind evaluation is to continually improve how you and your team define goals as well as how you carry out the actions needed to achieve them.

Reexamining goals midstream

As you work toward your goals, take the time to step back periodically and review them. Ask:

- Are they still *realistic*, given any changes in constraints or resources?

- Are they still *timely*; that is, is now the best possible moment to achieve them?

- Are they still *relevant*; for example, do they still align with the company's strategy?

But think carefully before modifying a goal midstream. Changing goals abruptly can create confusion for everyone who's striving to achieve them. Sure, if the organizational or external environment has changed and reaching a particular goal will no longer create value, it is certainly appropriate that you adapt by refining or removing the goal. Perhaps you jettison the goal entirely or change it to better reflect new business conditions.

On the other hand, you should not alter goals merely because you've encountered obstacles such as personnel changes or schedule slippage. As we've seen, if you've planned well, you'll have contingency arrangements in place for handling these obstacles.

If the time comes when you do need to change or jettison a goal, make sure to get buy-in for your proposed action from your team, from upper management, and from other key stakeholders before proceeding. That way, you'll all "be on the same page" with the change you've proposed.

Assessing goals after reaching them

Reaching a goal is exciting and satisfying. But it is not the end of the goal process. You still need to evaluate the goal's impact and consider whether you might be able to accomplish similar objectives more effectively in the future. To assess a goal after it's been reached:

- Confirm that others agree the goal was accomplished and the expected impact was achieved.

- Examine how the goal was achieved. Who did what? When? And how?

- Identify what worked well in achieving the goal and what you would change in the future. Record both lists of insights.

What Would YOU Do?

Eyes on the Prize

DON HEADS THE CUSTOMER service group within Eyes on the Prize Inc.'s customer relations unit. After completing performance appraisals for his direct reports, he meets with his group. He's pleased that his employees have reduced the average length of a customer service call. And he urges them to continue this effort, while maintaining quality and covering all the points in their telephone scripts. Don informs the group that the customer relations unit is being reorganized; as a result, they will be getting three new associates.

The next day, one of Don's direct reports, Jane, asks Don to review her goals for the coming year. They are:

1. Continue to reduce the length of her calls, with a goal of a 5 percent reduction.
2. Review her completed calls against the telephone script checklist.
3. Continue to train new customer service associates as needed.

Don mulls over how he might best respond to Jane's goals. He wonders to himself, "Should I tell her that her goals are 'right on'? What about asking her to make her training goal more specific, in light of our upcoming reorganization? Should I explain that I need to meet with everyone first to discuss the unit's goals, and only then refine individual goals?"

What would YOU do? The mentors will suggest a solution in *What You COULD Do.*

- Evaluate the payoff of achieving the goal. If the payoff does not meet your expectations, determine whether you overestimated the goal's impact.

- Communicate your evaluation of the goal to everyone involved.

- Identify issues you need to address next time; for example, defining goals more clearly according to the SMART criteria, creating better contingency plans for obstacles, or building more flexibility into projects required to achieve a goal.

Learning and applying lessons

Identifying lessons learned while working toward a goal is one of the most important benefits of the goal-evaluation process. Once you internalize these lessons, you can begin to apply them as you develop new goals or adapt existing ones for your unit, your employees, and yourself. For example:

- If you've decided that a goal was too easily achieved, work to make future goals a bit more challenging.

- If you believe that a goal took too much effort, try making new goals a little easier.

- If you suspect a goal was unrealistic, make sure that subsequent goals better reflect organizational realities and time constraints.

- If you noticed a skill deficit while your unit was pursuing a goal, decide how you'll ensure that people have the right capabilities and knowledge to achieve goals you'll define in the future.

- If team members lost motivation while working toward a goal, figure out how you might help them see the value of subsequent goals and how you might communicate about new goals in ways that inspire and motivate them.

By extracting lessons from each experience you have in setting and achieving goals, you can constantly hone this important managerial skill, not only in yourself but also in your direct reports.

What You COULD Do

> Remember Don's questions about how to respond to Jane when she presents three possible individual goals?

Here's what the mentors suggest:

Don should tell Jane that he first needs to meet with everyone to discuss the unit's goals. Before defining individual goals with each of his direct reports, he must clarify the overarching unit goals. The unit has just reorganized. He needs to find out and communicate what the unit as a whole wants to accomplish in the coming year. Only then can he determine which of his employees' objectives are most important and how individual goals might be refined to reflect and support the larger unit goals.

True, Jane's goals are a good start and do align well with Don's thinking. But for a group working closely together, with common objectives, it's important to align individual goals with the larger unit goals, which must in turn align with the organizational strategy and direction.

Tips and Tools

Tools for Setting Goals

Worksheet for Developing Goals

Use the following chart to identify goals in different work areas. After you have identified the goals and expected outcomes, assign a priority to them.

Role	Goal	Expected Outcome	Priority (A, B, C)
Supervisor	*Complete all performance evaluations within time frame set by human resources.*	*– Direct reports satisfied that performance evaluation is a priority. Feedback available in a timely manner.* *–No work pending to HR.*	*A*

Worksheet for Writing SMART Goals

Use this worksheet as a guide to writing SMART goals.

Part I : Identify your goal

Write your goal in the space below.

Part II: Is your goal SMART?

Evaluate the goal you listed above according to the SMART criteria. If you can answer yes to all of the following questions, your goal is SMART.

Is your goal . . .	Yes	No
Specific: Can you describe the details?		
Measurable: Can you measure the goal using either quantitative or qualitative assessments?		
Achievable: Can you achieve your goal?		
Realistic: Can you achieve your goal within the current environment, given existing constraints?		
Time-limited: Have you set a deadline for your goal?		
If you answered no to any of the criteria above, you may want to consider rewriting your goal. Rewrite your new, SMART goal in the space below.		

Worksheet for Creating Goals and Tasks

List the tasks associated with each of your goals and include the time frame, resources needed, potential obstacles, measured outcomes, and milestones for each task.

Goal:		
Payoff:		
Task 1:	Time frame:	Resources:
Obstacles:	Measured outcomes:	Milestones:
Task 2:	Time frame:	Resources:
Obstacles:	Measured outcomes:	Milestones:
Task 3:	Time frame:	Resources:
Obstacles:	Measured outcomes:	Milestones:
Task 4:	Time frame:	Resources:
Obstacles:	Measured outcomes:	Milestones:
Task 5:	Time frame:	Resources:
Obstacles:	Measured outcomes:	Milestones:

Worksheet for Gauging Obstacles/Solutions

Before you begin executing your tasks, list the potential obstacles. Identify the possible solutions and then evaluate how well your solution worked.

Goal:

Obstacle	Solution	Not Effective	Effective	Very Effective	Comments
		How Well Solution Worked			
Incomplete information	*Start anyway*		X		*In the future I will make sure that resources supply information before my start time. I prefer to work with more complete information.*

Worksheet for Evaluating Goals

After you have completed the tasks for a goal, use this worksheet to evaluate the goal.

Description of goal:

Briefly describe your goal.

Was the goal achieved?

If not, was the goal realistic? Or were there issues that led to the goal not being achieved?

Did the payoff meet or exceed expectations?

Explain.

Would you approach a similar goal the same way?

Explain.

Did you communicate your evaluation to all participants?

If so, how was it received?

Test Yourself

This section offers ten multiple-choice questions to help you identify your baseline knowledge of the essentials of setting goals. Answers to the questions are given at the end of the test.

1. In terms of importance, goals generally fall into one of three categories: critical, enabling, or nice to have. What is a key difference between a critical goal and an enabling goal?

   a. A critical goal must be accomplished in order for your unit to continue to run successfully. An enabling goal may not be essential, but it creates a more desirable long-term business situation or takes advantage of a new opportunity.

   b. A critical goal is a short-term goal that has emerged unexpectedly and overrides other activities. An enabling goal is created to resolve issues raised by the critical goal.

   c. A critical goal is a short-term goal that reflects the organization's mission and strategy. An enabling goal is a long-term goal originating from your business unit.

2. What are the two most common methods for goal setting?

   a. Brainstorming and directive.

   b. Top-down and bottom-up.

   c. SMART and SPIN.

3. How frequently should you set goals for your unit?

   a. Monthly.

   b. Quarterly.

   c. Once or twice a year.

4. To prioritize and select goals, you first rank your goals: A (high value and importance), B (medium value and importance), or C (little value and importance). What should you do next with your B-level goals?

   a. Rate each of them as A, B, or C and prioritize them accordingly.

   b. Determine whether they are short- or long-term goals.

   c. Break B-level goals into A goals or C goals, and eliminate the Cs.

5. You're developing a plan that will help your unit achieve its key goals. What is your *first* step?

   a. Determine what resources are needed to achieve your goals.

   b. Establish a time frame for the completion of your goals.

   c. Decide what specific tasks will have to be done in order to accomplish each goal.

6. How many of your own goals as a manager should be related to your unit?

   a. All of them.

b. None of them.

c. Many of them.

7. The research and development team has set a goal of making the company's software product easier to update. In the middle of its implementation, the lead programmer leaves to take a job in another firm. Which of the following should the team do *first*?

a. Stop work on the project until a new programmer comes on board.

b. Reassign the programmer's task and continue working on the project as planned.

c. Assess whether the project is still realistic.

8. Reaching your goal is not the end of the process. What is?

a. Celebrating the accomplishment.

b. Evaluating the goal's impact.

c. Creating a paper trail of the process used to reach the goal.

9. Which of the following is the best advice you can give a new manager who is trying to help set goals for her unit?

a. Aim low—it is better to achieve your goals than it is to challenge your team too much.

b. Start small—it is better to define several clearly manageable targets than one overly broad one.

c. Set ambitious goals that push your team to its limits—failing to achieve goals is fine as long as your team learns from the experience.

10. "SMART" is an acronym representing criteria for expressing goals in clear terms. What does the "A" stand for?

a. Applicable.

b. Accurate.

c. Achievable.

Answers to test questions

1, a. Critical goals are those that are crucial to your operation; they must be accomplished for your unit to continue running successfully. Enabling goals, on the other hand, create a more desirable business condition or take advantage of a business opportunity. They are important, but they fill a long-term rather than a critical need. An example of a critical goal is ensuring that order-processing technology works correctly. An example of an enabling goal is deciding to capitalize on a new fad to increase sales of a product.

2, b. In top-down goal setting, unit management sets broad goals, and each direct report sets goals that support those of the unit. In bottom-up goal setting, direct reports develop individual goals, and their manager integrates them into broader goals.

3, c. For most organizations, it is recommended that you and your team set unit goals once or twice a year. Your challenge during this process is to sort through all the potential goals that you could pursue and identify those that will create the most value for your organization.

4, c. While it makes sense to assign B-level headings on your first time through the list, the suggested next step is to break all B goals into A (worth your time) or C (not worth your time). Your list will now contain only top-priority goals.

5, c. Asking "What specific tasks do we have to complete in order to accomplish each of our unit goals?" is the first step toward achieving those goals. Some tasks you identify may need to be completed sequentially, so your next step will be to place the tasks you identify in order. Remember: if a task seems overwhelming, you can always break it into smaller parts.

6, c. While the majority of your goals will likely be tied directly to unit goals, components of unit goals, or goals that reflect your contribution to a team member's goals, you may also have some goals that are not specifically related to your unit. For example, you may want to serve on a task force to revamp companywide health benefits, even though that activity is not directly connected to the work done by your unit.

7, c. It is important to periodically assess whether your goals are still realistic, timely, and relevant. In this case, the programmer's departure may make this goal unrealistic for now. However, it is important not to alter goals too quickly in reaction to obstacles such as personnel changes or schedule slippage. Before you modify a goal midstream, carefully consider the effects of the change.

8, b. After reaching a goal, you need to evaluate the goal's impact as well as consider whether you might be able to accomplish similar goals more effectively in the future. Spending some time identifying what was successful and what was not will likely make your goal setting more productive the next time.

9, b. Starting with small, specific goals is a good way to both motivate your team and keep it on track. Many managers try to do too much too quickly and fail to focus on one or two sharply defined targets. It is nearly impossible to succeed when you establish vague or overly broad goals.

10, c. In addition to being *S*pecific, *M*easurable, *R*ealistic, and *T*ime-limited, a goal needs to be *A*chievable—not too difficult to be accomplished, and not so unambitious that it's accomplished too easily.

To Learn More

Articles

Allen, Peter. "Communicate to Set Up Strategy, Not Roadblocks."
Harvard Management Communication Letter, December 2002.

> Managers, take note. For employees to do their best work, they
> need to really believe that they matter to your organization—
> and to you. But building work relationships based on empathy,
> concern, and trust is easier said than done. People can learn to
> work productively together if they recognize they share com-
> mon goals. The path to that goal is authentic communication.

Brown, Tom. "Turning Mission Statements into Action." *Harvard
Management Update*, September 1997.

> Corporations love to author mission statements because they
> help an organization figure out its purpose and help employ-
> ees work toward that goal. But if management fails to create
> commitment to the statement, there can be no action toward
> realizing that statement. In order to make your mission state-
> ment a reality, you must complete five steps: (1) iteration,
> (2) awareness, (3) understanding, (4) commitment, and
> (5) action.

Carney, Karen. "Successful Performance Measurement: A Checklist." *Harvard Management Update*, November 1999.

Does your performance measurement system actually boost performance? Here's a checklist for ensuring meaningful performance measurement. Includes an annotated "If you want to learn more" section and a sidebar on "soft" metrics entitled "Measuring the Soft Stuff."

Kaplan, Robert S. "Target Setting." *Balanced Scorecard Report*, May–June 2006.

Articulating strategy and identifying strategic objectives often get the spotlight as major scorecard-building challenges. But defining measures and setting targets are no less challenging, for different reasons. And unlike the more stable Balanced Scorecard (BSC) elements, targets must, by definition, be continually revised. One of the most delicate tasks is setting effective stretch targets—those that are ambitious, yet achievable, without being demoralizing. The implications are great, not just for company performance but for individual performance and morale. Here, Robert S. Kaplan discusses external and internal benchmarks across the four BSC performance perspectives, presenting proven methods for setting stretch targets that deliver the results leaders want without incentivizing the wrong behavior.

Ledingham, Dianne, Mark Kovac, and Heidi Locke Simon. "The New Science of Sales Force Productivity." *Harvard Business Review*, September 2006.

Leaders who take a scientific approach to sales-force effectiveness have learned to use four levers to boost their reps' productivity in a predictable and manageable way. First, they systematically target their firms' offerings, matching the right products with the right customers. Second, they optimize the automation, tools, and procedures at their disposal, providing reps with the support they need to boost sales. Third, they analyze and manage their reps' performance, measuring both internal processes and results to determine their teams' strengths and weaknesses. Fourth, they pay close attention to sales-force deployment—how well sales, support, marketing, and delivery resources are matched to customers. These four levers can help sales leaders increase productivity across the board, the authors say, though they have the greatest impact on lower-ranked performers.

Books

Ferner, Jack D. "Setting Goals and Priorities." In *Successful Time Management: A Self-Teaching Guide*. New York: John Wiley & Sons, 1995.

This book provides a broad overview of the principles of time management. The author maintains that time management is a process that involves analysis, planning, and commitment. He includes exercises for incorporating the principles into everyday situations, both professional and personal.

Hammond, John S., Ralph L. Keeney, and Howard Raiffa. *Smart Choices: A Practical Guide to Making Better Decisions*. Boston: Harvard Business School Press, 1998.

Smart Choices blends the art and science of decision making into a straightforward, proven approach for making tough choices. *Smart Choices* doesn't tell you *what* to decide; it tells you *how*. Authors Hammond, Keeney, and Raiffa, among the world's best-known experts on resolving complex decision-making problems, blend the art and science of decision making into accessible steps that lead you to consider your choices both intuitively and analytically.

Rouillard, Larrie A. *Goals and Goal-Setting: Planning to Succeed*. Menlo Park, CA: Crisp Publications, 1993.

This book is designed to be read interactively. It contains a series of exercises, activities, and assessments designed to explore the value of goals and the importance of fundamental goal setting.

Wilson, Susan B. *Goal Setting*. New York: AMACOM, 1994.

This book deals with the fundamentals of goal setting. Part one is an overview of the goal-setting process. Part two covers goal setting and people skills—specifically how you can use effective communication to achieve your goals. Part three walks you through the steps of goal setting and achieving goals.

eLearning programs

Harvard Business School Publishing. *Influencing and Motivating Others*. Boston: Harvard Business School Publishing, 2001.

Have you ever noticed how some people seem to have a natural ability to stir people to action? *Influencing and Motivating Others* provides actionable lessons on getting better results from direct reports (influencing performance), greater cooperation from your peers (lateral leadership), and stronger support from your own boss and senior management (persuasion). Managers will learn the secrets of "lateral leadership" (leading peers), negotiation and persuasion skills, and how to distinguish between effective and ineffective motivation methods. Through interactive cases, expert guidance, and activities for immediate application at work, this program helps managers to assess their ability to effectively persuade others, measure motivation skills, and enhance employee performance.

Harvard Business School Publishing. *Managing Direct Reports*. Boston: Harvard Business School Publishing, 2000.

Learn the skills and concepts you need to effectively manage direct reports and be able to apply these techniques immediately to your own situation. Through interactive practice scenarios, expert guidance, on-the-job activities, and a mentoring feature, you will learn and practice how to:

- Understand direct reports' expectations
- Manage a network of relationships
- Delegate along a continuum

Pre- and post-assessments and additional resources complete the workshop, preparing you for more productive direct-report relationships.

Sources for Setting Goals

The following sources aided in development of this book:

Ferner, Jack D. "Setting Goals and Priorities." In *Successful Time Management: A Self-Teaching Guide*. New York: John Wiley & Sons, 1995.

Harvard Business School Publishing. *Creating Teams with an Edge*. Boston: Harvard Business School Press, 2004.

Harvard Business School Publishing. *Manager's Toolkit*. Boston: Harvard Business School Press, 2004.

Levinson, Harry. "Management by Whose Objectives?" *Harvard Business Review* OnPoint Enhanced Edition. Boston: Harvard Business School Publishing, 2003.

Matta, Nadim F., and Ronald N. Ashkenas. "Why Good Projects Fail Anyway." *Harvard Business Review*, September 2003.

Rouillard, Larrie A. *Goals and Goal-Setting: Planning to Succeed*. Menlo Park, CA: Crisp Publications, 1993.

Schaffer, Robert H. "Demand Better Results—and Get Them." *Harvard Business Review* OnPoint Enhanced Edition. Boston: Harvard Business School Publishing, 2000.

Wilson, Susan B. *Goal Setting*. New York: AMACOM, 1994.

Notes

Notes

Notes

Notes

Notes

Notes

How to Order

Harvard Business School Press publications are available world-wide from your local bookseller or online retailer.

You can also call:
1-800-668-6780

Our product consultants are available to help you 8:00 a.m.–6:00 p.m., Monday–Friday, Eastern Time. Outside the U.S. and Canada, call: 617-783-7450.

Please call about special discounts for quantities greater than ten.

You can order online at:
www.HBSPress.org